THE FACIAL EXPRESSIONS GLOSSARY

BUSINESS VERSION

Annie Särnblad

BOOK DESIGN BY SARAH MATTERN
sarahmattern.com

STUDIO PHOTOGRAPHY BY BARRY BRAUNSTEIN
barrybraunsteinphotography.com

ISBN: 979-8-9883819-1-4

To my students:
past, present, and future

Contents

Introduction | 1

Facial Expressions in Negotiations | 5

Expressions | 9

Introduction

For over a decade, I have taught facial expressions—the nonverbal and universal language of our species—to clients all over the globe, including Young Presidents Organization, Stanford University, NBC, The European House - Ambrosetti, and the Museum of Science in Boston. My workshops and keynotes are interactive, and "learning by doing" is my favorite way to teach.

All of the facial expressions I teach are hardwired into us humans. They present on our faces regardless of age, gender, socialization, culture, and geographic location.

Facial expressions are a teachable skill because we humans have biological responses to each individual emotion. Each emotion creates a *specific* and *different* change in blood flow and muscle movement in our bodies and on our faces. We are programmed to respond to facial expressions when we see them.

There is a reason each feeling *feels* different.

We sweat when we are nervous, cry when we are sad, wrinkle our noses when we find something to be distasteful. When we are frightened, our hands get cold. Our lips tighten when we are angry. When we are aroused, our blood moves to the middle of our bodies.

When you can read facial expressions, every face-to-face interaction with another person provides feedback. This feedback has changed the structure of my thought patterns in much the way that becoming fully multilingual has. It opens the door to both flexible thought and to seeing situations and humans exactly as they are, without a filter of translation. It also helps me learn what works and what doesn't when it comes to connecting with others and helping them solve their problems. Ultimately, it helps me to love well, and for this I am eternally grateful.

I hope by helping others to read expressions—and therefore emotions—correctly, we make the world a kinder, more connected, and more compassionate place for us all.

Indeed, it's harder to be crabby with other people when you can see that they are struggling.

What follows is a visual guide to the nonverbal and universal language of our species.

This glossary includes clean and marked up photographs of each facial expression, accompanied by descriptions. As you study these expressions, try making them yourself in a mirror to gauge what emotions you see and feel. Then compare your interpretations to the labeled photos and written descriptions. The practice of making expressions is needed for the brain to fully process and interpret them. *This is how we are wired!*

If you want to test yourself ...

Skip the glossary table of contents and look at each picture to see if you can determine the primary emotion (yes, some of them have hints of other feelings) and then turn the page to see if you got it right!

Note that this glossary includes both full and fleeting expressions. Full expressions contain all the pieces of the specific emotion on the face. They are also usually held for a bit. Duration and the wholeness of the expression make them easier to see. Fleeting or partial expressions can be harder to identify if your gaze isn't prepared, or if you don't understand the expression's primary location on the face.

I've worked for years with my daughters and son to identify what we consider the primary location on the face for each specific emotion. This has helped us identify expressions even when only using our peripheral vision—if you see a jump, or a sudden movement in the primary location of that emotion/expression, you can identify the feeling even when you have a less-than-clear view and your eye only catches a flicker or a jolt. We know, for example, that a jump on the chin is vulnerability, a flash of the white area in the eyes above the irises is fear, and a jolt next to the nostril is "No!" This has made family dinners at our house interesting, to say the least.

With enough practicing in the mirror, studying of the photographs here, watching other people's faces, and working with videos (look up my videos online), it is possible to actually feel an expression as it pops up on your face. To me, this feels like a tiny sting of electricity localized to a specific area of the face.

As for seeing expressions on others, get used to planting your gaze on the lower part of the face around the mouth or on the upper area of the face around the glabella (the space between the eyebrows). In particular, be ready to look at either of these areas when you know you want to gauge another person's reaction to something you're going to ask or say.

Personally, I favor watching the lower part of the face. Though I look at the entire face, I always go back and forth from direct eye contact to the area around the mouth when I'm talking to someone.

Note—do not stare more than three seconds at a time at someone's mouth while they are looking back at you. Their brain will tell them that you want to kiss them. I might have learned this the hard way. Ugh!

However, if their gaze is on another person and you are off to the side, you can look at their mouth area as long as you like.

Practice watching expressions in videos. Play, pause, rewind, watch in slow motion, and try watching without sound.

The studio photographs included in this book were shot by the exceptional Barry Braunstein. I've included a few of my own personal photographs for emotions that can be difficult to capture in a studio setting, particularly those such as unbridled joy, pleasure, happiness, love, relief, flirting, and desire. I've used real pictures for these because I can't make these expressions on demand—I need to actually be experiencing the emotion in the moment. For each of these photos, I remember exactly what I was feeling.

Facial Expressions in Negotiations

I grew up professionally in Asia and spent almost a decade in Singapore. My professional and personal relationships almost always overlapped, as is so common there. Over and over, I heard variations of, "Why would you ever want to work with someone if you don't know, like, and trust both them and their family?" I was taught by my Singaporean clients and business partners that there is only one "self," and that the idea of a split between the personal self and the professional self isn't a healthy one.

This perspective was shared by my expat friends and clients. Indeed, I often wonder if those of us who chose to stay in Singapore for so many years did so, in part, because it fit with our own "collective" wiring. I miss many of the people I worked with. I miss their families too.

In Singapore, I kept my ability to identify microexpressions secret. Only a handful of people outside my family knew *why* I could read people the way I could. I was able to go into high-stakes negotiations and quickly decode the intentions of each individual in the room. I could let my clients know who had unexpected alliances or deeper ulterior motives. I knew who was lying, who was sleeping together, and who simply didn't "get" the task at hand.

Today I teach my clients to see microexpressions themselves so they can improve their connections with others and protect their own businesses. Reading microexpressions is certainly a game-changer in negotiations, but ultimately it helps us even more in our personal lives. We humans need to feel seen and understood to feel truly loved.

Below are some of the specific expressions I teach clients to look for during negotiations, as well as where on the face to see these expressions and when in a meeting to pay extra attention. For further details on what each expression looks like, refer to that specific expression's marked up photograph and explanation later in this book.

Also note that one of the best tactics in a negotiation is to have two or more people who can read microexpressions on your team. This way the person talking or pitching doesn't have to focus both on what they are saying and on monitoring expressions. When multiple people are paying attention to the microexpressions, fewer emotions are missed and the debrief afterwards is richer and more nuanced.

Yes, No, Maybe So

The YES Face (Joy): True joy causes the cheeks to lose gravity and pop up. The rise of the cheeks pushes out the normally flat skin under the eyes (the area where we get dark half circles from lack of sleep). I call these bulges "smile bags." If the area underneath the lower eyelids is flat, an expression is not genuine joy, *even* if the mouth forms a huge smile.

In a negotiation, when you see someone's cheeks rise to make smile bags, the person is likely pleased with what just happened or what was just said. This indicates that the negotiation is going well and you are on the right track.

I try to use humor in negotiations and meetings if at all possible. Laughter relaxes us and increases our ability to focus and be present in the moment. Humans also tend to be more forthright about their needs and wants when they are comfortable and happy. In addition, likability is often one of the deciding factors when people choose whom to do business with.

I once was in a meeting where a client talked about the possibility of dying, and the potential investor raised his infraorbital triangles (the balls of his cheeks) in delight, which caused smile bags to show under his eyes. That broke the deal. Thank God.

The YES Eyes (Want): Another piece of YES is dilated pupils. Dilated pupils means: "I WANT THAT!" It shows excitement, greed, arousal, and desire. It indicates that the person wants more of whatever is on the table. It can be romantic, as in, "I'm so into you!"—or have to do with food, "I want to eat that right now!"—OR in a professional context, "YES, I want to move forward with this!" The pupils must dilate *during* the meeting in response to something said or done. Because dilation can happen so fast and we don't typically stare at someone's eyes during an entire conversation without looking away, gauge the size of the pupils at the beginning of the meeting and compare as you proceed with your pitch.

If you EVER see someone show arousal at someone else's pain: get out! Do not do a deal with them and instead carefully figure out how to get them all the way out of your life—away from your money, your employees, and your loved ones.

The NO Face: This is the "I don't want to" face. The NO microexpression is a little bunny rabbit twitch on one or both sides of the nose, right next to the nostril. I always do this on the left side of my nose. When you see this in a negotiation it means that the person showing it is uncomfortable and doesn't like something that just happened or was just said. When you are about to talk about price, scope, or partnership—plant your eyes on the bottom part of the other person's face so you won't miss this expression. Plan ahead so you're prepared to pivot and adjust if someone shows the NO Face.

We humans mirror expressions, so if you find someone making the NO Face repeatedly, you shouldn't be surprised if you start making it too. It doesn't help a negotiation move forward when both parties are growling at each other, so it may make sense to respond instead with kindness. Many times, I've been able to completely change the tone and dynamic of a meeting by repeating in my head, "Loving kindness, loving kindness." Even saying that silently to myself causes my cheeks to rise and softens my expression. People have a deep need to be liked, and you can be both savvy and kind in a negotiation. There are many different negotiation styles, but my preference will always be for peaceful resolutions where both sides are happy with the outcome.

In my experience, the NO Face is a much more common expression than anger, which is clearly identified by the tightening of the lips. Anger, of course, can also indicate that the negotiation is moving off track.

The Maybe Face: This expression means: "I'm not yet convinced ... I'm still not sure." If you see this expression in a negotiation, you have more work to do to show the other person that you can perform and deliver your product, service, deal, or promise. The Maybe Face pulls both corners of the mouth down at the same time. It's often long enough to see clearly and is commonly accompanied by a shoulder shrug and/or lift of the eyebrows. If you see this expression, ask questions, provide clarification, and exemplify how you are going to meet their needs.

I Can't Say and Uh Oh....

Holding Back: This is the expression of "I have something I NEED to say, but I'm exercising self control!" It's the facial expression equivalent to biting your tongue. It produces a large long bubble of skin popping out right below the lower lip. If you see this in a meeting, pull the person aside afterward and bring up the topic—in my experience they will almost always fill you in on what they were already itching to say. Usually, it's something they felt strongly about but didn't feel comfortable saying in a group setting. If you want to know what anyone is thinking in any given situation, just ask. I often feel that I get to know people and their priorities on a completely different level simply because I see and ask.

Oh Crap!: This is one of my favorite expressions, and it's extremely useful in a negotiation. It shows when and where the other party is unsure or anxious. If you see it, you should treat it seriously. For example, if you're asking an employee of a company you're planning on acquiring, "Will the technology be ready for market in four months?" And the employee answers, "Yes, of course," but shows the Oh Crap! microexpression ... well then, you may have a problem that needs further investigation. Consider it a red flag when facial expressions aren't aligned with words.

Microexpressions show where we need more information. Reading facial expressions turns every face-to-face interaction into feedback. You can use this feedback to improve your performance, your ability to connect on a deeper level, and your relationships. It matters to see and understand other people's wants and needs. At the end of the day, reading microexpressions correctly helps keep our hearts, our loved ones, and our businesses safer.

Expressions

If you want to test yourself...

Look at each picture to see if you can
determine the primary emotion
(yes, some of them have hints of other feelings).

Then turn the page to see if you got it right!

Guess the expression! Then turn the page. $\longrightarrow$

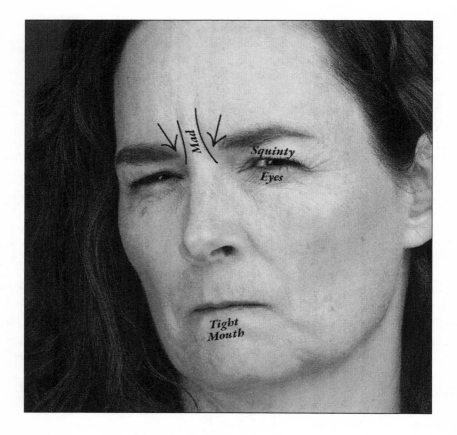

1. Anger

In this expression, the brows pull tightly toward each other and down toward the nose tip. Since this same brow movement exists in deep thinking, look for proof of anger in tight lips. Lips may also be pushed out like they are trying to grab at something, or they may be puckered and/ or closed tight—but either way, they will be TIGHT if anger is present. Anger may also be shown in bulging eyes or squeezed muscles around the eyes.

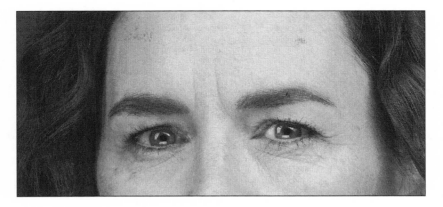

Guess the expression! Then turn the page. $\longrightarrow$

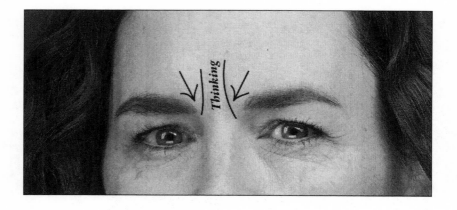

2. Deep Thinking (solving problems)

Deep thinking includes the same furrowed brow as anger—so the forehead looks identical, but the lips won't be tight. If the lips *are* tight, that's evidence of anger. A furrowed brow gives me wrinkles that I call my parentheses—I have two very clear, vertical lines that are visible even when my face is relaxed. These two wrinkles are etched into skin from years of repetitively making this expression. Some people only have one clear wrinkle between their eyebrows.

Guess the expression! Then turn the page. $\longrightarrow$

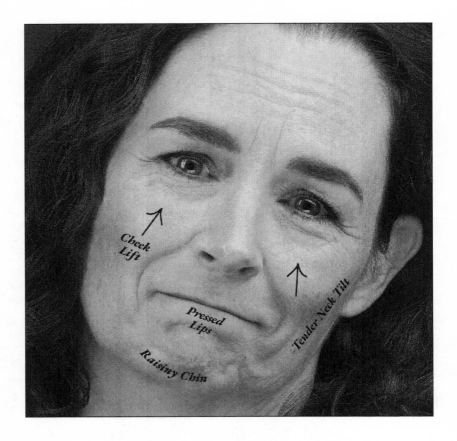

3. Empathy, Compassion, Kindness

Empathy, compassion, and kindness show in a puckered, raisiny chin accompanied by lifted cheeks. This is the look of "I see your pain, and I'm sending you support and kindness." Note that sometimes I also feel empathy in my heart and on my face simply by mirroring whatever expressions the other person is exhibiting. If they are angry, I may show anger on their behalf, etc. I often find myself nodding to show understanding as they are telling their story. This photograph shows extra softness in the tenderness of the head tilt.

Guess the expression! Then turn the page. $\longrightarrow$

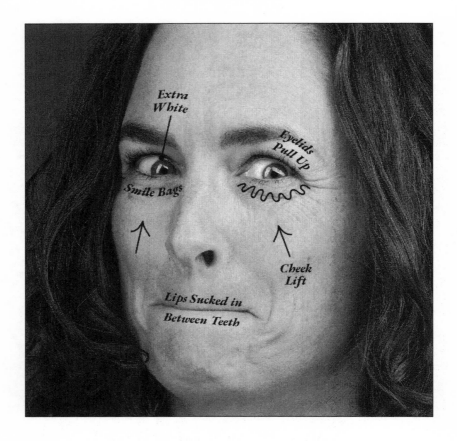

4. Excitement, Mischief

In excitement, lifted cheeks create smile bags under the eyes showing joy, and sucked-in lips show playful mischief. Both upper and lower eyelids pull up—BUT if the eyelids are pulled up *too* hard above the irises, this signifies fear—so, if the attempted excitement is disingenuous, it ends up signaling danger. (Think Hilary Clinton's expression when she tries to feign excitement. When the eyelids are pulled way up, and signaling fear is completely out of context, it makes people feel uncomfortable and like something is "off.")

Guess the expression! Then turn the page. $\longrightarrow$

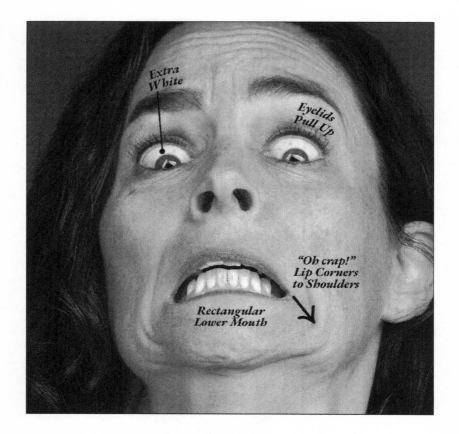

5. Fear

In fear, the lower lip forms a rectangle, the upper eyelids pull back to show the white space above the irises, and the eyebrows pull straight up. Fear makes the neck tendons jump, stretch, and pop. Whenever I see a jolt of neck tendons, I know it's fear. I find this to be one of the tells that is visible even with only peripheral vision.

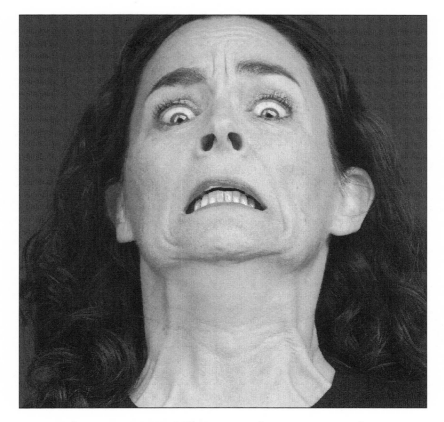

Guess the expression! Then turn the page. $\longrightarrow$

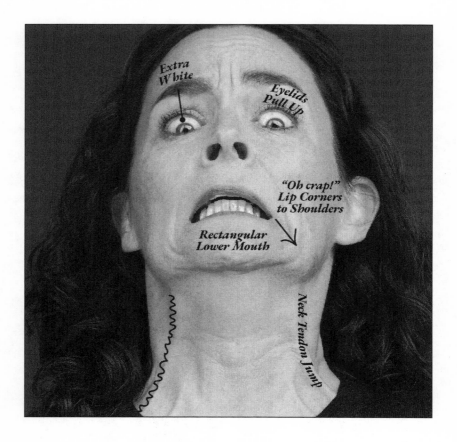

6. Fear (extreme)

In extreme fear, the lower lip forms an exaggerated rectangle, the upper eyelids pull *way* back to show the white space above the irises, the eyebrows pull straight up, and the neck tendons *really* pop out. This expression even goes so far as to flare the nostrils, which we sometimes do when we are preparing to fight.

Guess the expression! Then turn the page. $\longrightarrow$

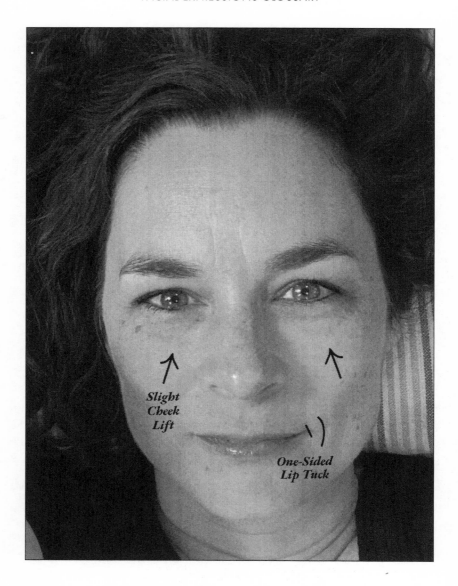

Slight Cheek Lift

One-Sided Lip Tuck

7. Flirty

When feeling flirty, the corners of the mouth can slightly raise, and one lip corner often tucks into the cheek. In this personal photograph, I'm trying to do a neutral expression, but I still have a bit of a knowing smile, as well as a slight intensity in the eyes.

Guess the expression! Then turn the page. →

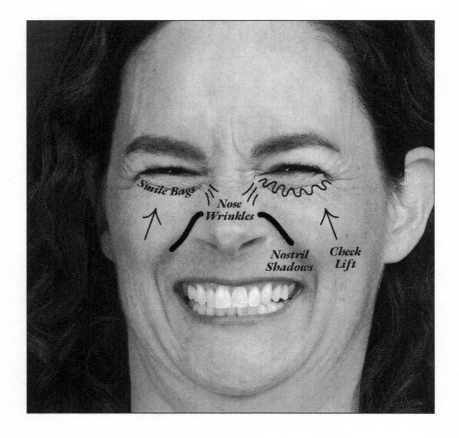

8. Funny and Inappropriate (the dirty joke expression)

This is a complex expression with two feelings presenting together to form an emotional sentence. Joy's raised cheeks and the resulting smile bags, combined with the NO Face's nostril shadows and squished wrinkles on the sides of the nose, express delight in the uncomfortable. This is the face I make, for example, when someone says something wickedly inappropriate and also very funny. The smile is slightly exaggerated here—probably because I was a bit uncomfortable making the expression on demand. That said, this expression usually has a piece of "awkward" in it, so that's not a bad thing!

Guess the expression! Then turn the page. $\longrightarrow$

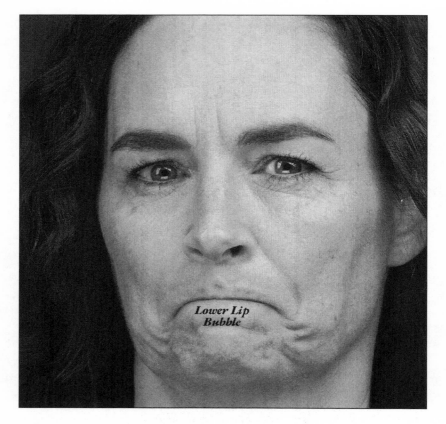

Lower Lip Bubble

9. Holding Back

This is a big expression, rather than a small or fleeting expression. There's a bubble below the bottom lip—what I sometimes call the Nordic chewing-tobacco bubble, because when I lived in Sweden, I knew a few people who, instead of tucking their chewing tobacco under their top lip, would tuck it between their lower teeth and lower lip. It takes effort to get the lower lip to pull in and down, and the chin has to move up to force out that bubble of skin (don't confuse the resulting chin pucker with vulnerability). This is the grown-up version of a child holding their hands over their mouth so they won't leak a secret. Think of it as the, "I have something to say and am bursting to tell you, but I don't want to get in trouble" look. In my experience, a person with this expression will usually share their thoughts once they are in a more comfortable environment—since they are already itching to say it!

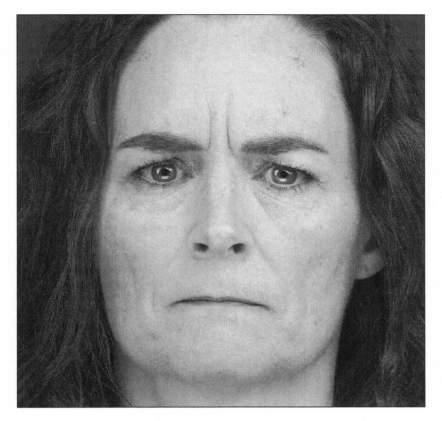

Guess the expression! Then turn the page. $\longrightarrow$

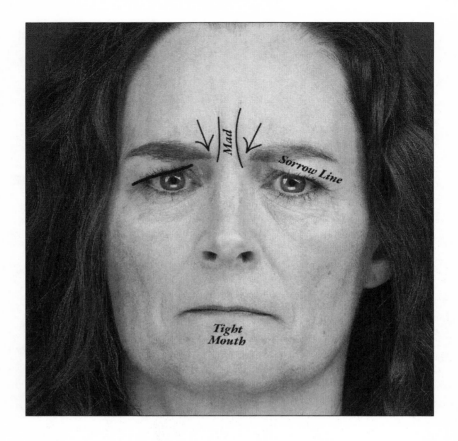

10. Hurt

The facial expression of hurt includes the sorrow lines and puckered chin of sadness and vulnerability, along with the furrowed brow and tight mouth of anger.

Guess the expression! Then turn the page. $\longrightarrow$

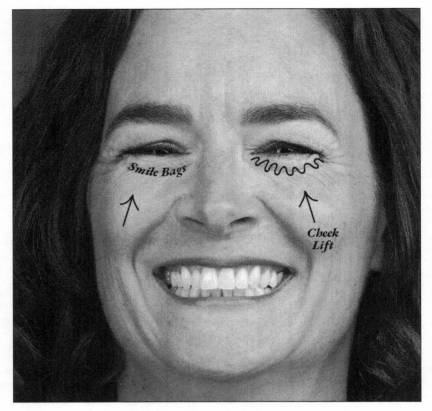

11. Joy, Pleasure, Happiness (the YES Face)

In real joy, the cheeks lose gravity—they rise and push the skin under the lower eyelids out because it has nowhere to go. This bulging occurs in the area underneath our eyes where we get dark circles from fatigue. I call these smile bags, and they are usually accompanied by a shadow under the bulge of skin that looks like a sideways crescent moon.

It is my stout and firm belief that we humans attach more to others who show their smile bags often. It is ironic that so many people want to do away with their smile bags and remove them from photos, when really they are one of the most attractive pieces of human expression. Simply put, happiness is healing and appealing, and showing our humanity is beautiful.

Guess the expression! Then turn the page. $\longrightarrow$

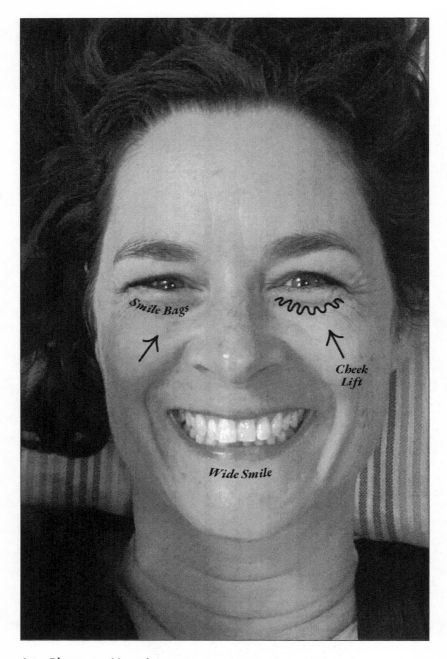

Joy, Pleasure, Happiness

Guess the expression! Then turn the page. $\longrightarrow$

Joy, Pleasure, Happiness

Guess the expression! Then turn the page. $\longrightarrow$

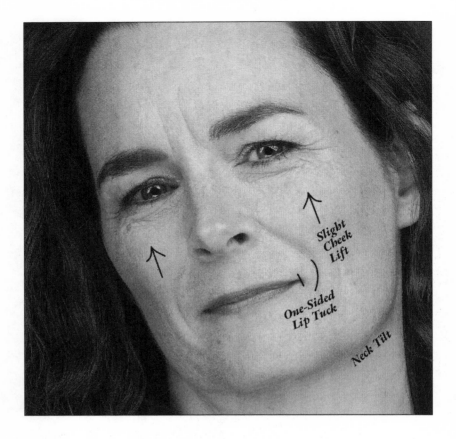

12. Knowing Smile (kind)

"I know something I think you don't know I know." (Yeah, I know!) This is a one-sided smile that has a soft, often kind or even loving look if the cheeks are raised. I also call this the Mona Lisa smile. It's often made in a discussion where someone is talking about something that the other person is well versed in. When it appears in flirtation, there will be other indicators, such as raised cheeks, lowered eyelids, and/or dilated pupils—in that case, it can also be interpreted as the "I know what you want, Baby!" look.

38

Guess the expression! Then turn the page. ⟶

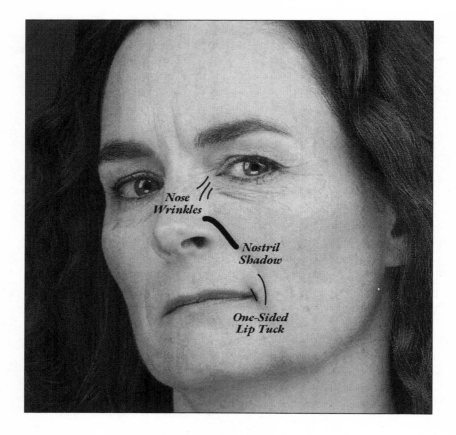

Nose Wrinkles

Nostril Shadow

One-Sided Lip Tuck

13. Knowing Smile (sinister)

This smile is similar to the knowing smile in that it has one lip corner tucked deep into the cheek—but the sinister knowing smile ALSO has a nostril shadow. It is the nostril shadow that turns this expression into one of ill intent. The nostril shadow will present on the same side of the face as the tucked lip. If you have a hard time catching the nostril shadow in a fleeting expression, trust your gut. Did it feel creepy, dirty, or unkind? If so, then it is a sinister knowing smile.

Be careful—particularly if the sinister knowing smile is accompanied by kind words. A facial expression that is the opposite of a person's words shows deception. Think of a fairytale where an evil character has a sinister expression while saying "come hither" words. Be wary! The sinister knowing smile can show predatory intent.

Guess the expression! Then turn the page. $\longrightarrow$

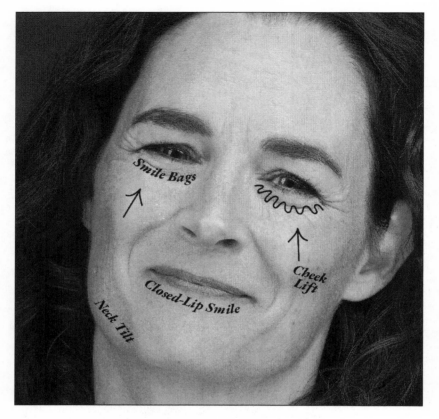

14. Love (affection) A

This is the affectionate love smile. I make this expression when I'm with the people I care deeply for. It can simply express a soft, platonic love, as in the photo above, and have none of the additional elements that are present in romantic love. Romantic elements would include pupil dilation, half-masted eyelids, and flushed skin. In both affection and romance, the love smile has a head tilt and a soft lift of the cheeks, which pushes out smile bags under the eyes and pulls up a gentle, closed-lipped smile. It may also include a puckered chin showing vulnerability—I do this expression often when I look at my children and feel that time is moving too fast. The puckering is hard to see in this expression because of the stretching of the chin from the smile piece. Sometimes there is also a soft, downward *contrasting* pull of the lip corners almost like in mirth—as if love carries with it a soft secret.

Guess the expression! Then turn the page. $\longrightarrow$

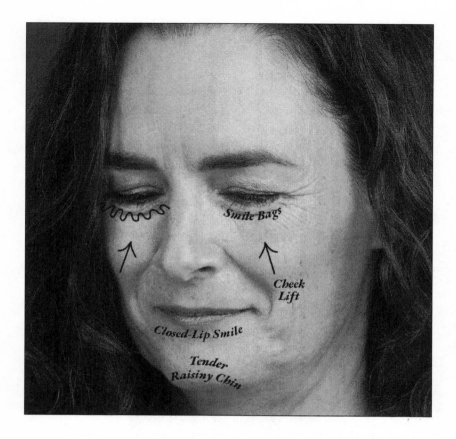

15. Love (affection) B

This picture of affection shows the same closed-lip smile as in the Love (affection) A photo, as well as a tender puckered chin, a soft lift of the cheeks, and smile bags. The eyelids are slightly closed, the chin is tucked, and the gaze is focused on the object of affection—a photograph of my children.

Guess the expression! Then turn the page. ⟶

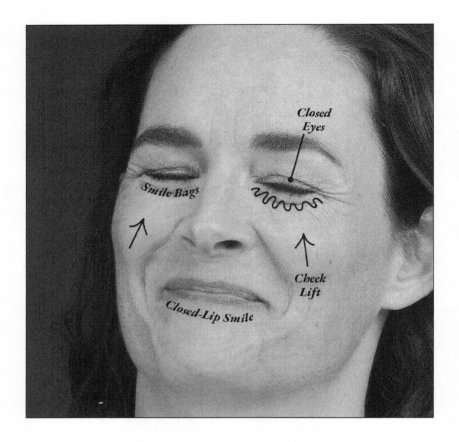

16. Love (affection) C

This picture of affection shows the same closed-lip smile as in the A and B photos, including a tender puckered chin, a soft lift of the cheeks, and smile bags. The eyelids are closed, and the chin is lifted in slight amusement.

Guess the expression! Then turn the page. $\longrightarrow$

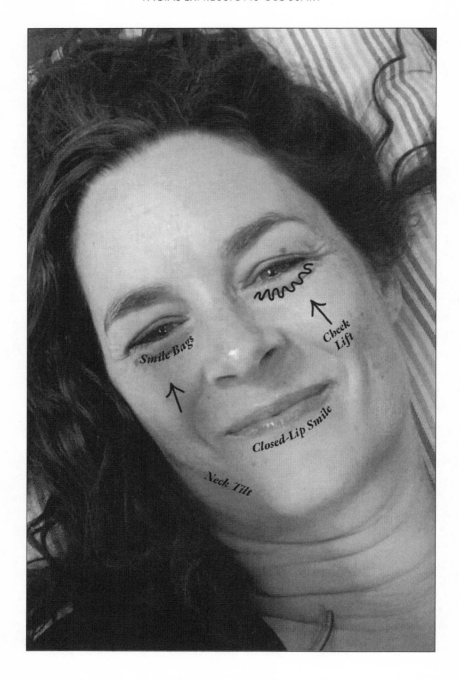

17. Love (romantic)

This is a complex expression that I believe is almost impossible to fake. All the pieces together build a paragraph of romantic love, which, when authentic, is a combination of joy, vulnerability, softness, flirtation, and arousal.

A gentle tilt of my head shows a willingness to be soft and vulnerable. My eyelids are relaxed and lowered in flirtation and desire. There is joy expressed in my raised cheeks and bulging of the skin under my lower eyelids. My "love smile" shows in my closed lips, which are stretched from the upwards-and-outwards pull of my cheeks. The love smile always feels *soft*, and when I make it on my own face, it floods my body with endorphins. It was bright when this picture was taken, so my impression is that my pupils are somewhat dilated, though it's hard to tell.

Another piece you should look for in this expression is the chin puckered in tenderness. That's harder to see with a smile, but proves that the emotion is strong and there is a willingness to be vulnerable. Look also to see if the skin is flushed with arousal—a flush is likely associated with desire if you see the skin color change in front of you, accompanied by pupil dilation and half-masting the eyelids.

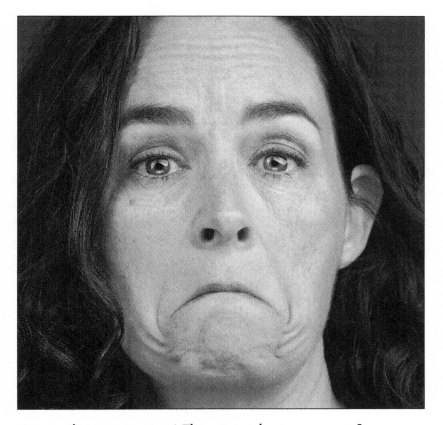

Guess the expression! Then turn the page. $\longrightarrow$

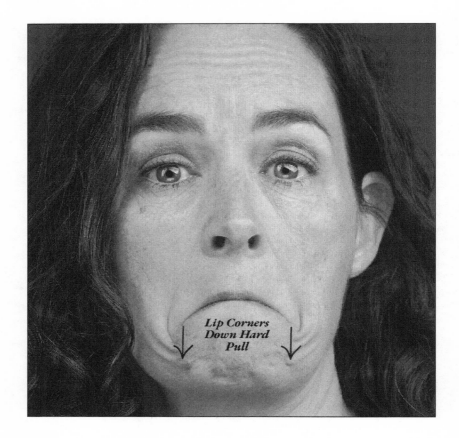

Lip Corners Down Hard Pull

18. Maybe (hmmm, will think about that)

In this closed-lipped expression, both lip corners pull down quickly and simultaneously. I often feel a slight jutting-forward of my lower jaw and teeth when I do this expression. It's a big expression rather than a fleeting one. It may express, "Hmmm, let me think about that." So if you're giving a business pitch and you see this expression, it's an indicator that you still have more work to do to convince the other person. I've also seen this expression when it means, "Wow, not bad, I'm impressed!" In that case, it's often accompanied by nodding and words that convey approval.

Guess the expression! Then turn the page. $\longrightarrow$

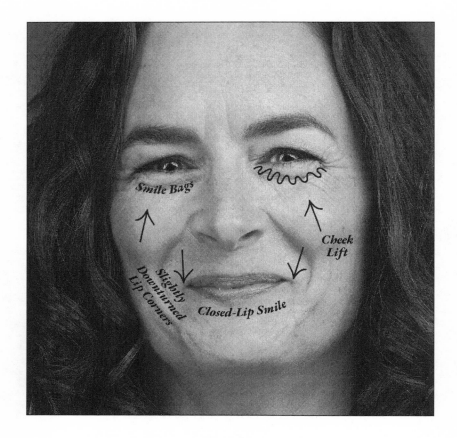

19. Mirth

In this expression, there's a *slight* downturn of both lip corners (I would also define this as "sass"—my eldest does this expression often), combined with a lift of the cheeks in pleasure that pull up a closed-lipped smile. It may also have an added slight *tricksy* element shown by a wrinkling and squishing of the nose (wrinkles on the middle part of the nose on both sides).

Guess the expression! Then turn the page. $\longrightarrow$

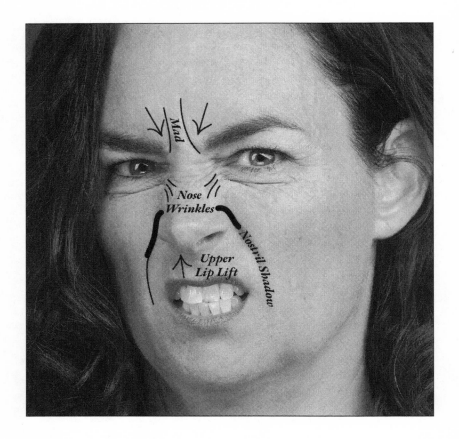

20. The NO Face

This is the "Ew face," the "I'm-uncomfortable-and-don't-want-to" face. Look for the nostril shadows at the top of the nasolabial folds (the lines that run from the nostrils diagonally down to the lip corners). Sometimes the nostril shadows form a clear line that looks like upside-down fish hooks that curl around the top of the nostrils and in toward the center of the nose. This expression can also have a raised upper lip on one or both sides of the mouth—the quintessential look of disapproval that is used particularly among mean girls in the United States. The NO face also often has a "scrunched nose," with wrinkles on one or both sides of the nose.

Guess the expression! Then turn the page. $\longrightarrow$

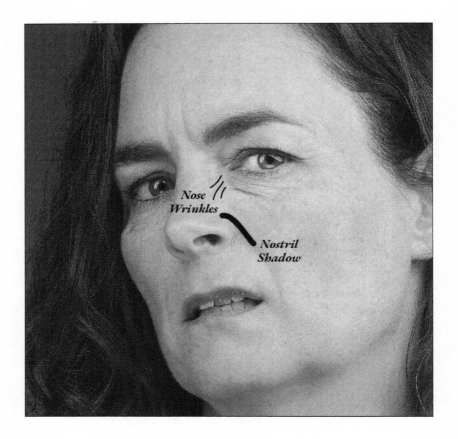

21. No (fleeting)

This is a fleeting expression of the NO Face, which has a quick jump/jolt upward of the skin on one side of the nose. This creates wrinkles next to the nose, as well as a nostril shadow and an upward pull of the lip on that side of the face. I always do this expression on the left side of my face, but this varies from person to person.

Guess the expression! Then turn the page. $\longrightarrow$

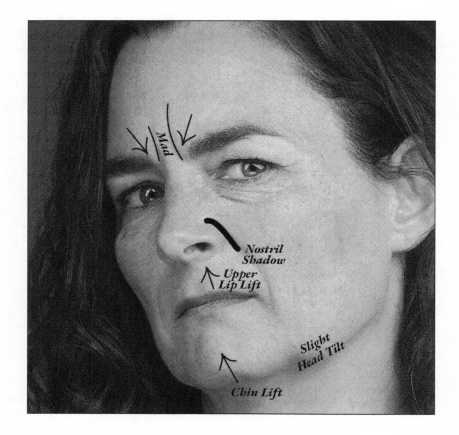

Mad

Nostril Shadow

Upper Lip Lift

Slight Head Tilt

Chin Lift

22. No (of disapproval)

This expression of disapproval includes the furrowed brow of anger, the nostril shadows and lifting of the upper lip of the NO Face, and a chin lift with a slight jut of judgment.

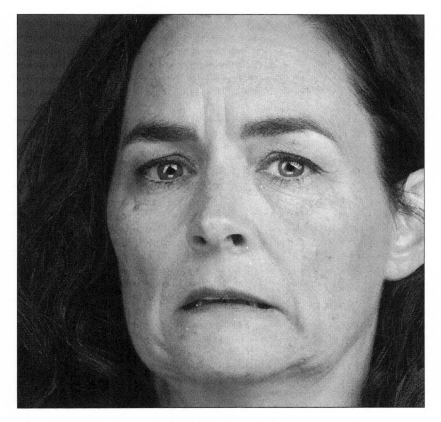

Guess the expression! Then turn the page. →

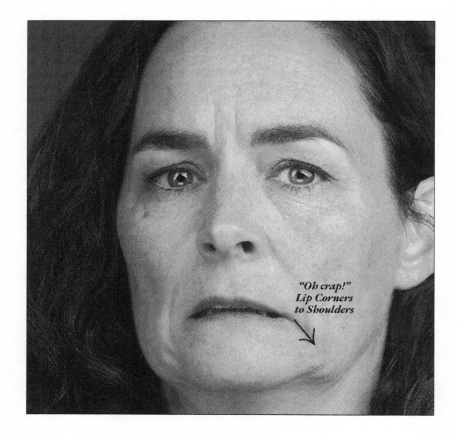

"Oh crap!"
Lip Corners
to Shoulders

23. Oh Crap!

In the "Oh Crap!" expression, one or both lip corners pull diagonally down to the respective shoulder, often accompanied by a sucking inhale (that sounds like a reverse hiss). We make this face when we receive worrying information, for example if someone gives you a deadline that you think you can't meet. If you see someone making this face when you ask for help with something, you should ask more questions to get to the bottom of what's going on. When I train people for high-stakes negotiations, especially in mergers and acquisitions, I tell them to watch for fear when asking about deliverables. If, for example, someone is saying they, "absolutely will have the product ready for market by X date," and they show fear, their face is indicating they don't actually believe what they are saying.

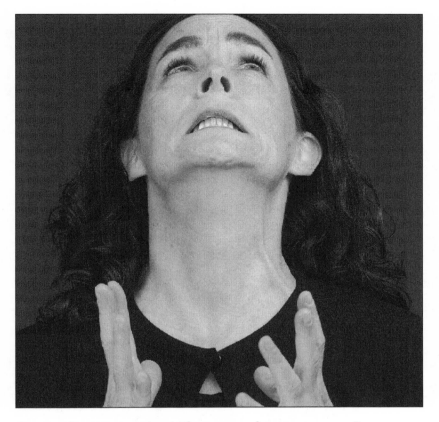

Guess the expression! Then turn the page. ⟶

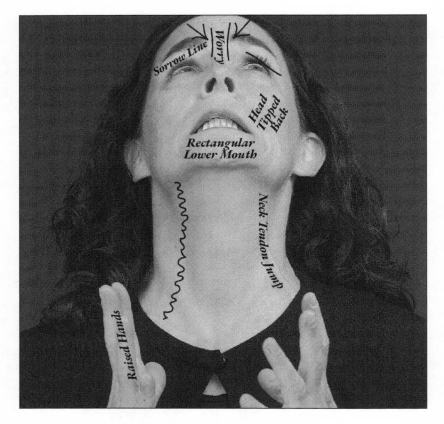

24. Pain, Anguish, Grief

Physical and emotional pain both have pieces of sadness in the raisiny chin and triangulated eyebrows, and pieces of fear in the rectangular lower lip and jump of neck tendons. Pain has an element of fear because pain not only hurts, but also *feels* permanent in the moment. Pain has a furrowed brow, showing a worried attempt to solve the problem. This complicates the expression by pulling down the inner edges of the eyebrows that are simultaneously trying to lift from sadness. The result is a chaotic, wrinkly mess with ripples going every which way. In extreme grief, there is often a lift of the head toward heaven and a raising and stretching of the hands as if praying to God. True grief is deeper than what I'm showing here, but my brain is probably relieved to not be fully immersed in the emotion—I know from experience that my body would believe the trauma message, and it would take me at least a day or two to recover.

Guess the expression! Then turn the page. $\longrightarrow$

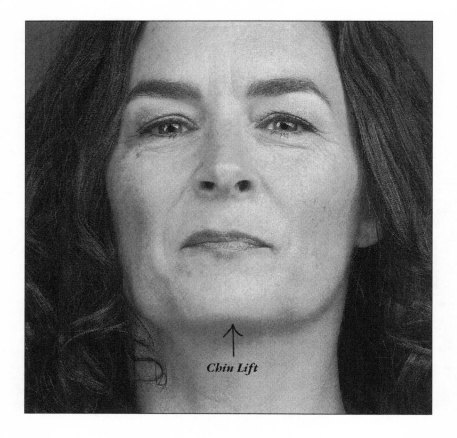

Chin Lift

25. Pride

In pride, the chin thrusts up and forward, sometimes accompanied by the lifted cheeks of joy. In this photo, I have a bit of a mirthy mouth with a close lipped smile that has the lip corners pulled slightly BOTH up and down. Defiance is similar to pride, but in addition to the chin lift, it will also have elements of other expressions, like pieces of anger, the nostril shadows of the NO Face, or the raisiny chin of vulnerability.

66

Guess the expression! Then turn the page. $\longrightarrow$

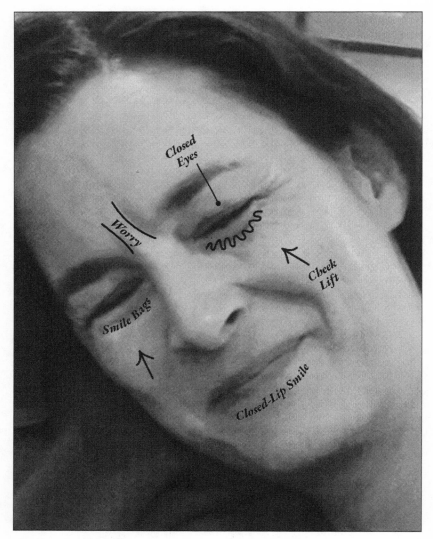

26. Relief

Relief lifts the cheeks in happiness and puckers the chin in vulnerability. In this photograph, the lines between my eyebrows are still furrowed from worry, and my eyes are shut, closing out the world to fully marinate in the emotion. The corners of my lips are pulled at once up and down, as is common in a soft, affectionate, platonic love smile. Note that worry and thinking both use the same muscle movements. I use context, including analyzing my own feelings in the moment, to differentiate between the two.

Guess the expression! Then turn the page. $\longrightarrow$

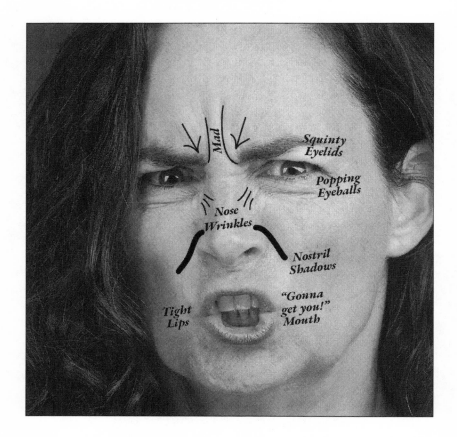

27. RUN! Face

This is a complex expression that shows that someone is ready to hurt another person. I used to demonstrate this while training my kids when they were little. No matter who made this face, my kids knew this expression meant they needed to *RUN!* because this person was likely to assault them. A furrowed brow, squinty eyelids, and popping eyeballs all show anger. The nose wrinkles, lifted lip, and nostril shadows show the NO Face. Tight lips with a "gonna get you!" mouth that reaches out toward the intended victim show extreme aggression. Try making this face and see how it makes you feel—it's truly awful.

Guess the expression! Then turn the page. $\longrightarrow$

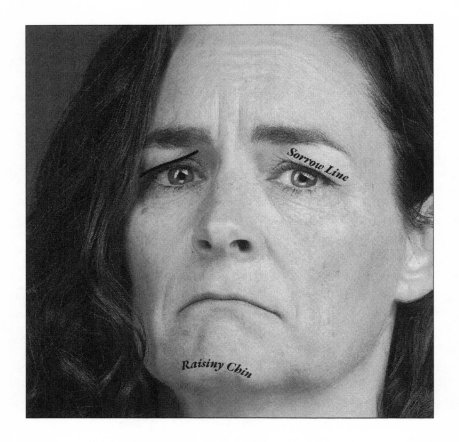

28. Sadness

The expression of sadness includes the squeezed chin of vulnerability and sorrow lines. Sorrow lines stretch from the inner eyebrows down to the outside corners of the eyelids. In sadness, the inner eyebrows often raise, although in this picture, that doesn't show because my eyebrows are furrowed slightly from worry.

72

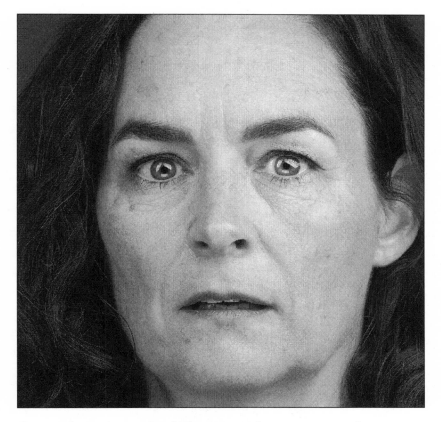

Guess the expression! Then turn the page. $\longrightarrow$

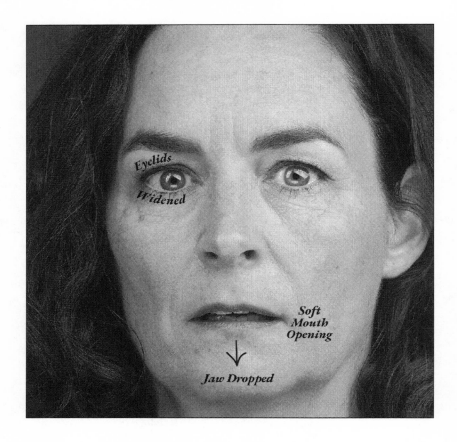

29. Surprise, Shock

Surprise differs from fear in that all its pieces are rounder. The eyebrows are softer in their "rise." The mouth and eyebrows are both "O" shaped. The chin drops and looks like the person forgot to hold their jaw shut. Shock (not shown here) has a widely stretched open mouth.

Guess the expression! Then turn the page. $\longrightarrow$

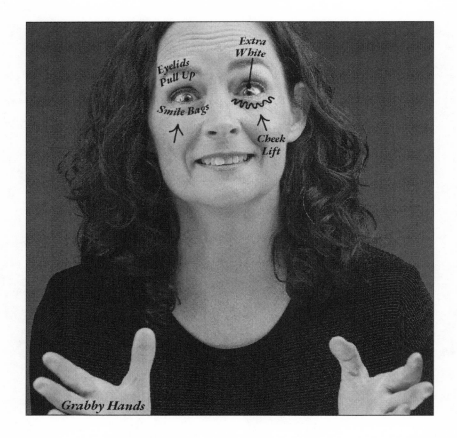

30. Volatile A

This picture shows a lift of the cheeks, usually present in joy, and a pulling back of the upper eyelids to show the whites above the irises, which is usually an element of fear. The reason this picture feels unsettling is because joy shouldn't be accompanied by fear. The grabby hands make this all the more uncomfortable.

If I see someone making repetitive expressions of the eyes of fear combined with a multitude of other expressions, I consider this a red flag. My hypothesis is that this person may be in a volatile state. I recommend that you think of people you've seen in the media, as well as in your own life, who make this expression so you can form your own conclusions.

Guess the expression! Then turn the page. $\longrightarrow$

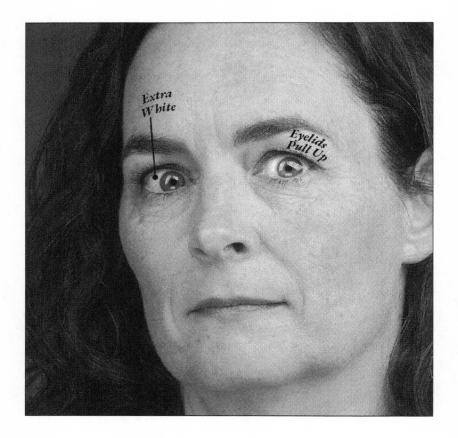

31. Volatile B

This is the expression of fear and should be shown in the context of fear. If someone is making this expression on a daily basis when there is no apparent danger, I believe there is a possibility that this person is exhibiting emotional volatility. Again, think about the people you know in the media and in your own life and draw your own conclusions. My hope is that learning to read facial expressions will make you more aware of what's going on around you.

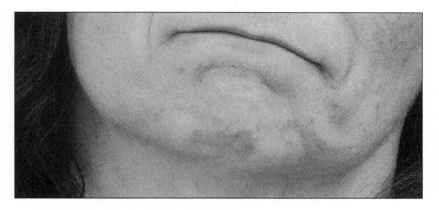

Guess the expression! Then turn the page. $\longrightarrow$

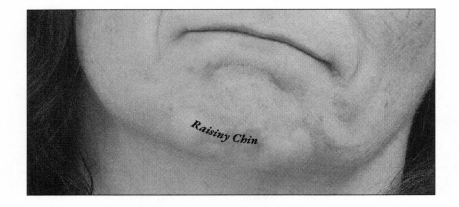

32. Vulnerability (tender)

With tender vulnerability, a squeezed chin turns the grape of the chin into a tight, dented, and puckered raisin. This creates tiny dimples, or as one of my clients says, "cellulite on the chin." This chin clench is present in **love, tenderness, empathy, and sadness**—indicating that there is a feeling of loss or the possibility of loss—"*I'm vulnerable.*" To practice this chin, first squeeze your butt muscles. Now do the same with your chin muscles. Yup, I find this funny.

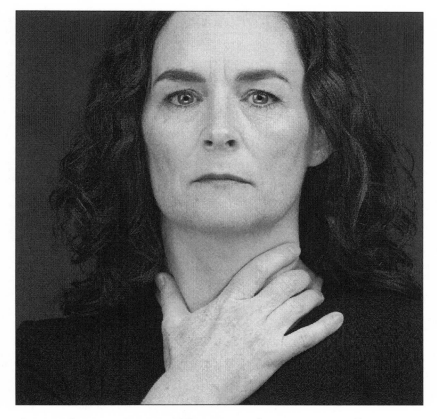

Guess the expression! Then turn the page. $\longrightarrow$

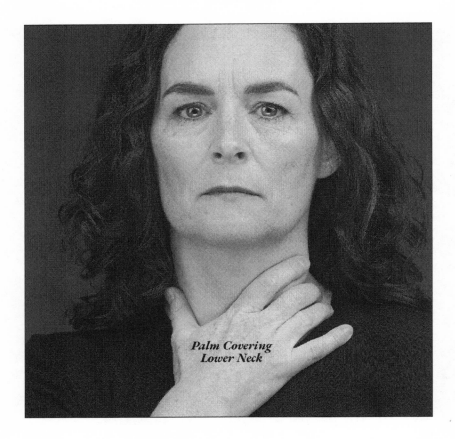

*Palm Covering
Lower Neck*

33. Vulnerability (feeling unsafe)

This is a particularly telling gesture, which I'm including because it's universal. Like all the facial expressions I teach, it exists irrespective of language, culture, upbringing, and socialization. The expression of feeling vulnerable and unsafe is shown by covering the neck with one hand.

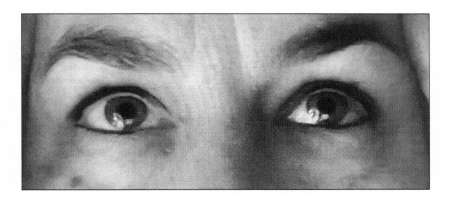

Guess the expression! Then turn the page. ⟶

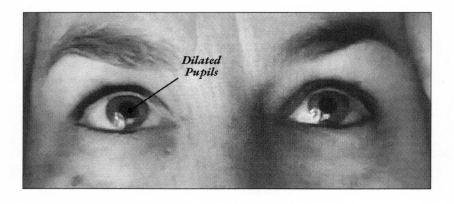

Dilated Pupils

34. Want, Greed, Desire (the YES Eyes)

Want, greed, and desire are shown in the swelling of the pupils. Our pupils also dilate from other stimuli, such as light and medication. To make sure you are assessing pupil dilation correctly, look for an increase in pupil size in real-time and in response to something said, seen, or reacted to. In every encounter, I gauge how big the other person's pupils are at the *beginning* of our meeting, and then I watch to see if there is a change during our conversation. This is especially useful in business negotiations and romance. In both cases, pupil dilation is an indicator that the person is highly interested in the task at hand. Pupil dilation in business can straight-up express "Give me that!" in response to a pitch or offer. It doesn't necessarily mean attraction to another person—it can simply mean I want what you just offered (money, chocolate, status, etc.). Context is everything!

References

My preference when choosing terminology is more playful than scientific. This is how my brain works—it's what sticks for me, and therefore what I can teach effectively. My work and process tend toward the pragmatic rather than the scientific, and I can't imagine sitting in a laboratory conducting experiments. I do, however, love mischief and am comfortable saying something comedic and outrageous to a stranger to elicit an expression I'm "working on."

Much of what I teach comes from the years I have spent studying language after language in immersive situations. My stubborn brain decided that if I had been born in a different country, I would have spoken that language perfectly—so I believed the key to learning languages was to remove my English completely and start with a clean brain slate.

Put simply, I have spent years of my life not understanding the spoken words around me, years of using facial expressions and body language to interpret intent, years of observing facial movements and coming up with my own interpretations of what these movements meant. All the while paying attention to every jump, jolt, twist, lift, push, and squeeze on my own face. I learned to listen deeply to what my own face whispers to my brain and my heart, and I still wake from dreams in the middle of the night and freeze my face mid-expression while reaching for something to write on before the insight and expression is lost. Yes, I am strange, as humans so often are. And yes, my obsession, like many other peoples' obsessions, is born from trauma.

My children have also put their own words on expressions, and I use many of these in my teaching. Lea, Emma, and Matthias are my laboratory, and I am theirs.

All this to say, I am entirely responsible for my own interpretations and chosen vocabulary, and it is my belief that some of the things I teach significantly transgress what has been proven in the scientific community. Certainly, it is possible that others would disagree with some of the expressions I teach and the methodologies I use. And, though I do not know what others would think of my simplifications, translations, and thorough reliance on my own face and feelings to decode expressions, I do indeed lean heavily on the experts in the field of facial expressions whose work has so deeply inspired me.

Therefore, I would like to express my sincere gratitude to the behavioral scientists whose research and writings have been invaluable to me and so many others. I wouldn't be able to do much of what I do without the individuals that have dedicated decades of their lives to decoding and identifying facial muscle movements and expressions.

Each of these behavioral scientists has worked tirelessly and followed established scientific methods to put words on what was previously considered invisible or even non-existent, and each has endeavored to document, translate, and teach others.

When I give keynotes, I refer to Charles Darwin and his book, *The Expression of the Emotions in Man and Animals*, which he published in 1872. We humans are hardwired in our facial expressions, and humans have written about facial expressions for as long as humans have been writing. However, Darwin paid *particular* attention to facial expressions and took great care in categorizing and documenting them. I like to think that we both experienced some of our aha moments under the same circumstances and in the same ways, in our travels over and over to foreign lands where we didn't know the language. When language isn't accessible, the brain switches on and lights up areas of seeing and understanding that would otherwise be ignored. When that happens, eternal patterns begin to emerge.

When I've taught in church, I've called my talk, "God's Language." It is my belief that facial expressions are the foundation that God has given us upon which we build verbal languages. The words we use and the names and sounds we humans invent vary, but I believe our original, nonverbal language is God-given and holy.

Carl-Herman Hjortsjö is one of the earlier 20th-century researchers of facial expressions. Hjortsjö was a Swedish anatomist who worked at the Swedish University where I did my undergraduate and graduate degrees, the University of Lund. He was methodical in his categorization of facial expressions. I read his work a long time ago in its original Swedish but lost interest when repeated rumors surfaced that he was racist.

Over the years, I've heard many whispers about different systems and ways of categorizing facial expressions, including that some countries, law enforcement agencies, militaries, etc. have their own methods. My guess is that the field has advanced in many places and in many ways, including AI, that I don't know about. How could this not be the case, given the human thirst for knowledge and that this is the universal language of our species?

Ultimately, I view learning to read facial expressions as a teachable skill that should be accessible to young people who value kindness and who want to live connected, meaningful lives. People who want to be good at loving and protecting both others and themselves. In my heart, that's what all this is for.

Current Experts and Leaders in Facial Expressions

Thank you from the bottom of my heart to the following modern leaders in the field of facial expressions. I encourage my readers to partake in any and all books, papers, and other teachings by the following experts:

Paul Ekman, who has deeply inspired me, and who has developed the largest and, in my understanding, the most thorough body of work in the field of macro- and microexpressions. He's brilliant and specific, and he has committed his life to meticulous scientific research that he so generously shares. In my view, he has changed the world. I'm eternally grateful to him, as well as to **Wallace V. Friesen** for authoring the "Facial Action Coding System" (FACS) in 1978, and for later updating FACS in 2002 along with **Joseph Hagar**. This pioneering body of work has given scientific legitimacy and structure to the field.

David Matsumoto is an expert, researcher, and teacher of facial expressions who has made significant contributions to the field.

Finally, I would like to thank **Erika Rosenberg**, who taught me FACS. Erika is brilliant, knowledgeable, and deeply committed to teaching and moving the field forward in groundbreaking ways. Words cannot express my gratitude.

Body Language

In my experience, the people who are the very best at body language are those who have a background in the military, or CIA, FBI, MI6, etc., and who have both received high-level training *and* used these skills in life-or-death situations.

While it's certainly possible to learn these skills in other ways, body language is notoriously fiddly—making it all too easy for self-proclaimed experts to make generalizations that someone with real training and experience can poke holes in, especially someone who is multilingual and multicultural, since so many aspects of body language are *not* universal.

Years ago, when I read **Joe Navarro's** material, I remember waiting for him to get something wrong—something where I've observed the opposite in my twenty-five years of living in foreign places ... He didn't. He kept getting it right. In particular, I love what he says about lie detection, about feet and torso "tells" in body language, and about how humans self-soothe by touching their skin in different ways. If you want to learn more about body language, I recommend you start with him.

About Annie

Annie Särnblad is a preeminent global speaker and expert in reading facial expressions, as well as an esteemed strategic advisor. She has developed her own, easy-to-absorb teaching techniques for facial expressions based on the knowledge she accumulated living in nine countries and studying eight languages through immersion. She is also certified in the Facial Action Coding System (FACS).

After leaving her hometown of Glencoe, Illinois on a Rotary Scholarship at the age of sixteen, Annie spent twenty-five years living outside her native United States across Asia, Europe, and Central America. She earned a Masters in Cultural Anthropology and started her career as a strategic advisor to Fortune 500s, startups, and family offices. She spent two decades coaching CEOs and management teams and sitting in on high-stakes negotiations.

Annie's clients currently hire her as a strategic advisor and/or for microexpressions training for their businesses. She has taught workshops for 4,000+ CEOs and Managing Directors all over the globe. Her clients end up finding her coaching transformative in both their professional and personal lives.

Although Annie is certified in FACS, she doesn't use FACS in her teaching, and her methods differ greatly from those of other experts in the field of nonverbal communication. This is because much of what she learned about facial expressions and nonverbal communications stems from spending many years of her life living and working abroad, studying languages through immersion, and so often not understanding what the people around her were saying.

Her unique teaching vocabulary and methods were developed during the trial, error, and aha moments of working with her children to recognize, translate, and simplify the expressions they saw on the faces around them as they lived on three continents. Annie's obsession with teaching her children facial expressions was born from her childhood trauma and deep need to keep her kids safer than she was. Survival instincts illuminate parts of the brain that would otherwise remain dormant.

Because children learn best when learning is fun, Annie's teaching methods involve interactive elements, as well as poking, prodding, and play.

As it turns out, humans are humans, and the learning techniques that work well for kids also work delightfully well for grown adults, especially people in positions of immense power who often have little time and short attention spans.

Learn more at **anniesarnblad.com**.

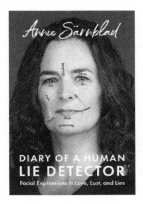

Made in the USA
Columbia, SC
20 February 2025

54087130R00059